PRAIRIE ANIMALS

Explore the Fascinating Worlds of . . .

BISON
by Cherie Winner
Illustrations by John F. McGee

HAWKS
by Wayne Lynch
Illustrations by Fred Smith

PRAIRIE DOGS
by Marybeth Lorbiecki
Illustrations by Wayne Ford

WILD HORSES
by Julia Vogel
Illustrations by Mike Rowe

NORTHWORD PRESS
Chanhassen, Minnesota

Photography © 2004:
Claudia Adams/Dembinsky Photo Assoc.: p. 43; Paul & Joyce Berquist: pp. 98, 112, 132-133, 135;
Jim Brandenburg/Minden Pictures: pp. 6, 10-11, 16-17, 26-27, 32-33, 36; Dominique Braud: pp. 102, 108, 116, 124,
151, 165, 168, 172, 175, 176; Richard Day/Daybreak Imagery: pp. 50, 63, 64, 66;
Tim Fitzharris/Minden Pictures: pp. 44-45; Jeff Foott: pp. 7, 20, 29; Michael H. Francis: cover, pp. 4, 22-23, 34-35,
36, 38-39, 41, 52, 92, 99, 110-111, 119, 120-121, 125, 129, 142, 148, 155, 156, 157, 161, 166, 178-179, 180, 183, 184;
Henry H. Holdsworth: pp. 8, 46; Donald M. Jones: pp. 53, 59, 74-75, 77, 83, 88, 118;
Gary Kramer/garykramer.net: p. 69; Bill Lea/BillLea.com: p. 153; Tom & Pat Leeson: pp. 14, 18, 31;
Wayne Lynch: pp. 58, 61, 62, 68, 76, 78, 81, 82, 84, 86-87, 89, 90-91;
C. Allan Morgan: pp. 72-73, 104, 105, 106-107, 138; Ted Nelson/Dembinsky Photo Assoc.: p. 13;
Dennis K. Olivero: pp. 96, 100-101, 115, 123; Jeff Vanuga: pp. 56, 126, 144, 145, 158-159, 162, 171, 182;
Shin Yoshino/Minden Pictures: pp. 15, 25, 37.

NorthWord Press
18705 Lake Drive East
Chanhassen, MN 55317
1-800-328-3895
www.northwordpress.com

Library of Congress Cataloging-in-Publication Data on file

Printed in Malaysia
10 9 8 7 6 5 4 3 2 1

PRAIRIE ANIMALS

TABLE OF CONTENTS

Explore the Fascinating World of . . .

BISON

Cherie Winner
Illustrations by John F. McGee

YOU KNOW what bison look like. You've probably seen pictures of them, like the ones in this book. Maybe you've even seen some live bison.

Now imagine looking out your window and seeing bison, nothing but bison, as far as you can see. That's what North American Indians and early pioneers saw.

In the 1700s, bison ruled the prairies! They roamed from northern Canada to Texas, and from Utah to Illinois. They traveled in groups called herds. Even small herds had thousands of members. Other herds had up to 4 million bison. If all the members of a big herd had lined up one behind the other, they would have reached all the way across the country and back. And that's just one herd!

Even within a large herd, bison keep in touch with one another and move as a group.

One early pioneer thought bison had a hump like a camel, a mane like a lion, and a beard like a goat.

In the winter, bison may regularly cross icy streams in their search for food.

Scientists who study animals are called zoologists (zoe-OL-uh-jists). They estimate that by the late 1800s, fewer than 1,000 bison remained in their prairie habitat, or home. The vast herds, all those millions of bison, had been killed for their horns, hides, meat, and sometimes for sport.

The bison that survived were scattered all over North America. A few people who cared about bison brought them together to breed them. These efforts saved the bison from becoming extinct, or dying out.

Today, between 10,000 and 15,000 bison roam wild. About 350,000 bison live on ranches, no longer wild animals. They are raised for their meat.

Bison were often called buffaloes by the early settlers, and the nickname is still used today. But true buffaloes are relatives of the bison that live in Africa and Asia, the cape buffalo and the water buffalo. Only North American buffaloes are bison.

Their scientific name is *Bison bison*. They belong to the bovine (BO-vine) family, along with cattle, sheep, and goats. All of these species (SPEE-sees), or kinds, of animals have horns, feet with two toes, and a stomach with four chambers.

Bison
FUNFACT:

Two of the largest wild bison herds today live in Wyoming's Yellowstone National Park and Canada's Wood Buffalo National Park.

Pages 8-9: Just after dawn and before sunset are good times for bison to feed.

Bison are one of the biggest members of their family. In fact, they are the largest land animal in North America. They are bigger than elk, bigger than moose, bigger even than the fearsome grizzly bear.

Indians had much love and respect for this huge animal that provided them with many things. They ate bison meat, made clothes and tepees from the hides, and made tools from the bones. In honor of the mighty bison, many Indian tribes made good luck drawings on rocks and cave walls called pictographs (PIK-toe-grafs) and petroglyphs (PEH-troe-glifs).

Male bison are called bulls. They may stand up to 7 feet (2.1 meters) high at the shoulder. They are 10 to 12 feet (3 to 3.6 meters) long from the tip of their nose to their rump, and they weigh up to 1 ton (2,000 pounds, or 909 kilograms). That's bigger than some sports cars!

Female bison are called cows. They are a bit smaller than bulls, standing about 5 feet (1.5 meters) tall at the shoulder. They measure 7 to 8 feet (2.1 to 2.4 meters) long, and they weigh about 800 pounds (364 kilograms).

Both bulls and cows have "beards." They usually grow longer with age, but scientists aren't sure of their function.

Bison are not only big, they have dangerous weapons. Both cows and bulls have two black horns that grow out of the skull above the eyes. They first grow out to the side and then curve upward and inward. The tips are usually very sharp. Horns grow throughout the bison's lifetime. They are never shed, or dropped off.

Horns are made of the same material as human fingernails, but they are much thicker and stronger than fingernails. There is a core of bone inside each horn near the head.

The bison has a flat face and short snout, or muzzle. Its horns may be as wide as 2 feet (61 centimeters) from tip to tip.

Bison use their horns in several ways. Sometimes two bison "lock horns" and push each other back and forth, in a kind of shoving match to see which one is stronger. At other times a bison sweeps its head back and forth, using its horns to slash at the belly of its opponent.

If a predator, or enemy, such as a grizzly bear attacks a bison, the bison might slash it. Or the bison might charge at the predator with its head down so its horns can gore, or stab, the attacker. Bison are fierce fighters. Usually, it takes two or more predators working together to kill an adult bison. If some of them attack from the front while others attack from the rear, they might bring down the bison.

Some people say bison seem to be wearing pants, or "pantaloons," because of the shaggy, long hair on their front legs. These bison are shedding their coats.

When herd members are startled or frightened they can suddenly take off in a sprint, almost as fast as a horse.

But in order to attack a bison, predators have to catch up with it first. And that isn't easy, because bison are very good runners.

Even though their legs look short, their top speed is about 35 miles (56 kilometers) per hour. And they can keep going at that speed for more than an hour.

Early hunters quickly learned that their horses could run faster than bison over a short distance, but they could not keep running for as long. If the hunters didn't catch up to a bison within a half-mile (0.8 kilometer) or so, they never would.

Bison have a large hump over their shoulders that makes them look clumsy and slow. In fact, the hump helps them run. Inside the hump is a strong muscle that holds up the bison's huge head. It also helps the front legs reach out farther, for a longer stride.

This bison head is so shaggy, you can barely see the horns. But the hump on its back is very clear.

A bison coat is unique. It has long, shaggy hair on the head, legs, and front part of the body, but very short hair on the back part. It looks as if the animal got a haircut that started at the back end and stopped in the middle! Bison also have a thick, brown beard of hair hanging from their chin.

The coat is thickest in fall and winter, to protect the bison from freezing temperatures and icy winds. The warm coat was often used as a blanket by settlers and Indians.

In spring, as the weather becomes warmer, bison shed their heavy winter coats. They look scruffy with big patches of loose hair hanging from their sides. Losing their fur makes bison itch. And to make things worse, mosquitoes seem to arrive at about the same time.

Bison use their tails like whips to shoo the insects away, but they still get bitten, and that makes them itch even more. Imagine having dozens of mosquito bites all over you, and no hands to scratch them!

But bison are not completely helpless when they itch. They scratch themselves by rubbing against any large, sturdy object, called a head rub. It might be a tree, a big rock, or even a building. But on the prairies, or plains, head rubs aren't very common. When a good one is found it is used by many bison. In fact, they may rub so hard, they scrape the bark off trees and knock down fence posts.

In Kansas in the 1800s, people tried putting sharp spikes into telegraph poles so bison would stop rubbing on the poles. But the plan backfired. Bison loved them! The spikes made great back-scratchers.

Another way bison can scratch themselves is by rolling in a wallow. This is a bowl-shaped depression in the ground. Most wallows are 8 to 10 feet (2.4 to 3 meters) across and about 1 foot (30.5 centimeters) deep. Some are much larger. Bison make a wallow by digging up the dirt with their horns, then lying down and rolling and kicking. They stir up a lot of dust.

For a bison on the prairie in the hot summer sun, a dust bath is like a natural bug repellent.

And if the wallow is wet, such as after a big rain, the bison come out of it covered with mud. They look like a complete mess, but the layer of mud prevents insects from biting them.

Once a wallow is made, many bison use it. Some wallows are visited by bison for many years, growing larger over time as more and more bison find them. All across the plains, large wallows could still be seen decades after bison had disappeared from the region.

Wallows are one sign that bison have been in an area. Other signs are their droppings, or scat, and their tracks. Fresh bison droppings are round, flat, and gooey. They look like a mushy Frisbee lying on the ground. After they dry in the prairie sun, they don't smell too bad. And that's good, because Indians and pioneers burned these "buffalo chips" to heat their homes and cook their food.

The track left by a bison's foot, or hoof, looks like two fat bananas facing each other. Each side of the track is made by one of two toes. The whole hoofprint is round and measures about 5 inches (12.7 centimeters) across.

At one time, people thought Indians and pioneers built their roads to follow bison paths. We now know that the herds did not usually make trails. They spread out and covered a wide area as they traveled.

Occasionally the bison did stay on a narrow path where they crushed the grass as they walked, and formed a "buffalo road." But these paths usually didn't go straight. Instead, the bison zig-zagged their way across the plains. And that wouldn't make a very good road!

Bison
FUNFACT:

The skin on a bison's neck and head may be up to 1 inch (2.54 centimeters) thick. Indians made shields of this tough skin.

A herd may spend several hours each day eating.
Because their bodies are so large they need lots of food for energy.

In their wandering, bison usually do not go to the same places every year. Even if they do, they usually take different routes than they have used before.

Bison move around so much to find food. They are called herbivores (HERB-uh-vorz) because they eat only plants, mostly grass. On the plains it may look as if the grass never ends. So why would bison have to go looking for more food? If bison lived alone, they wouldn't have to travel as much. But they live in herds. And when thousands of bison come to an area, they quickly eat and trample the grass. Then they have to move on, to find more food.

The whole herd may move 10 to 15 miles (16 to 24 kilometers) in a day. In pioneer times a herd would travel hundreds of miles in one year. Today, with fences and towns blocking their way, bison can't go nearly as far as they once did. But they still roam.

During their travels, bison don't follow a pattern. They don't move north in the spring and south in the fall as many birds and other animals do, for example.

Bison just wander. Sometimes they follow the scent (SENT), or odor, of fresh grass. Sometimes they go where they found good food once before. And sometimes they keep moving until they happen to find a new source of food.

A herd could be just about anywhere at any season. Even the Indians, who knew bison well and depended on them for almost everything, rarely knew exactly where they would be.

When bison find an area with fresh grass, they stay for a few days. Eating grass and other vegetation is called grazing. If the weather is very hot, bison graze during the cooler times at dawn and dusk, and sometimes even at night. If the weather is not hot, they might graze through the afternoon as well. Once or twice a day they go to the nearest stream or pond to take a long drink. Then they return to the grazing area.

Bison
FUNFACT:

From 1913 to 1938 the U.S. minted over 1.2 billion nickels with a bison on one side. They are rare today. Bison are also found on stamps in many countries, including the U.S., Canada, Germany, and Russia.

Wading in streams or ponds is a good way to cool off.

Sometimes herd members move close together as they travel across the prairie. At other times they stay farther apart.

Bison are ruminants (ROO-mih-nunts), which means their stomach has four chambers. They chew their food several times to get all the nourishment they can from it. Bison have no upper front teeth, so when they grab a mouthful of grass, they snip it off with their sharp side teeth. Then they grind it up with their large back teeth, called molars. When they swallow it, the food enters a large chamber of the stomach where bacteria begin digestion.

Bison may graze for an hour or more at a time. Then they find a comfortable spot where they can lie down and rest. They bring up a wad of grass they swallowed earlier, called their cud, and chew it again. They swallow that mouthful, bring up another wad, and chew some more. Finally the meal is finished. It then passes to other chambers of the stomach, where digestion continues.

Bison
FUNFACT:

Birds sometimes line their nests with hair that bison have shed. It may be as long as 24 inches (61 centimeters) if it comes from the bison's head.

A group of grazing bison looks very peaceful. As some of them graze, others rest in the shade, chewing their cud. But bison are always alert for danger to the herd.

Bison don't see very well, but they have good hearing and a sharp sense of smell. When they sense danger, their ears prick up and their tail lifts. They also may make grunting and snorting noises to signal other members of the herd.

Sometimes, bison ignore a passing intruder such as a wolf or mountain lion. Other times, if the intruder seems ready to attack, they will challenge it. The bison paw the ground with their front hooves. They move closer, lowering their heads so their horns point forward. This warning is often all it takes to make the intruder back down and leave the area. But bison will fight if necesary, to protect themselves and the herd.

Even while grazing, bison are always alert to any danger that may be nearby.

If bison are startled by a sudden danger such as fire or a loud storm, they often stampede (stam-PEED). In a stampede, the whole herd races off at a full gallop. They may run for miles, not even stopping to see whether they are still in danger.

This behavior sometimes made bison easier to hunt. Indians would surprise groups of bison to make them run toward a cliff called a "buffalo jump." The stampeding bison would be running so fast that by the time they saw the cliff, they couldn't stop. Over they went, falling to their death on the rocks below. The Indians then took the bison meat and hides for their families.

If a danger is not sudden enough to make bison stampede, they move away from it more slowly. The leader of the group, usually an old cow, decides when the group should move on. She walks or trots away from the danger, and the rest of the group follows her. They keep going until she decides it is safe to stop.

Bison don't need shade to be comfortable when they rest and chew their cud. They often just lie down near more food.

A herd is made of several smaller groups, or bands. Each band has from three to fifty members. As a herd spreads out to graze, each band stays together, but they leave space between one band and the next.

Each band includes females of all ages, their babies, or calves, and their offspring from previous years. Young bulls may stay in the band until they are four years old. Then they travel and eat on their own or with other bulls in a separate bachelor (BACH-ler) group.

Bison
FUNFACT:

From a distance, a stampeding herd sounds like thunder or a big waterfall. Some people say the ground even shakes like an earthquake.

Bison are social animals. They usually prefer to gather in groups.
But on the wide-open prairie they may wander away from the herd.

During the rut, competing bulls slowly approach each other, lower their heads, and raise their tails. Then they charge at full speed again and again until one gives up.

In late summer the breeding season, or rut, begins. Bulls start visiting bands of cows. They look for mates and try to keep other bulls away.

The bulls make a deep, loud, roaring sound called a bellow (BEL-oh), to warn other bulls to leave. They stand sideways to each other, to show how big they are. They lock horns and try to shove each other out of the way. Sometimes they fight, cutting and poking each other with their sharp horns.

Bulls also show off in the wallows. The biggest, strongest bull rolls in a wallow first, showing by his kicks and rolls how tough he is. After he leaves, all the other bulls take a turn in the wallow as the cows watch.

Sometimes bulls are so busy with these battles that they don't eat much, so they lose weight. They may also become wounded, but there is a reward. The bull that wins the rutting contests will mate with several cows. Bulls that lose these challenges probably won't mate at all that year.

The winning bull follows his group of cows for several days or weeks. He knows when a cow is ready to mate by sniffing her urine. As he sniffs, he lifts his upper lip. That lets the scent enter a special organ, called the Jacobson's organ, in the roof of his mouth. This organ is very sensitive to the chemicals in the female's urine that tell the bull she is ready to mate.

After the bull has mated with all the cows in his group, he and the cows separate again. The females go back to their band. The males go back to the bachelor group, where they can heal the wounds they received during the rut.

All of the bison must prepare for the coming winter. They must store fat to help them get through the cold months.

Bison fur is thick and repels water. It may look soft, but it actually feels rough. A bison tongue is very sensitive in choosing good grasses to eat.

Not even early snowstorms stop bison from finding
the precious food that will help them stay strong until spring.

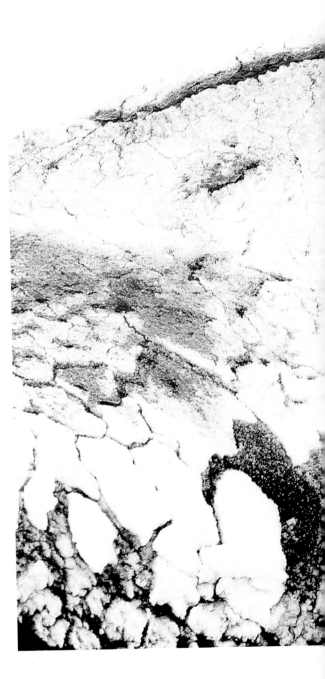

If they can eat enough before winter comes, and if the snow isn't too deep, bison survive winter very well. They may seek shelter among trees or in the hills. Their thick coat helps them stay warm. To reach grass under the snow, they use their broad snouts to sweep aside the snow.

Icy winds that seem harsh to us actually help bison by blowing snow off the ground, so the grass is easier to see. Deep snow makes food harder to find, and it makes travel more difficult. Bison can't move very fast if they have to wade through snow up to their bellies.

Bison
FUNFACT:

At the start of winter, bison have a layer of fat nearly 2 inches (5.1 centimeters) thick on their back. By spring the fat is gone.

A bison's coat acts like a protective blanket.
The cold doesn't get in, and the bison's warm body heat doesn't get out.

Calves usually nurse for about 6 months. Mother's milk is high in protein and fat, which gives the calf lots of energy.

But even the most severe winter eventually comes to an end. The snow melts, the days grow longer and warmer, and the grass grows tall. This is the world that greets bison calves, which are born sometime between April and June. Each cow usually has one calf. Twins are very rare.

A newborn bison looks different from its parents. Its fur is reddish and it does not have a shoulder hump. It weighs between 30 and 70 pounds (13.6 to 31.8 kilograms) and is quite strong. Within a half-hour it can stand up. It begins to nurse, or drink its mother's rich milk. In a few days it is able to keep up with its mother and play with other calves.

A calf stays close to its mother for about 1 year. She protects it and teaches it many things to help it survive.

Bison mothers probably recognize their own calves by their smell and the sound of their cry, called a bleat (BLEET). But calves don't seem to recognize their own mother. If a cow and calf become separated, the calf will follow any large animal it sees, including another bison, a horse, or even a person.

This calf has a lot of catching up to do
if it is going to grow as large as its mother.

Crossing a stream or river in a group may help protect
each bison against the hidden current.

The first few months of a bison's life are very dangerous. If a calf wanders away from its mother and the rest of its band, it may become a meal for predators such as wolves and grizzly bears. Nearby bulls sometimes help calves by standing guard over them and scaring away predators.

Calves also face danger when their band crosses a river. Adults are good swimmers and don't fear the water. But a young calf may be lost if the current is swift.

A calf that escapes these dangers grows quickly. In September its shoulder hump begins to develop, its coat starts to turn dark brown, and little bumps appear on its head where horns are beginning to grow. It still nurses, but it also eats grass and sometimes other plants, as the adults do.

One of this calf's horns is starting to appear just above its eye, and its coat will soon begin to darken. These are sure signs that it is healthy and growing.

During the winter the calves huddle with their mothers and other adults, learning how to stay warm and find food.

When spring arrives, the calves are called yearlings. They are like teenagers. They have grown a lot, now weighing about 350 pounds (158 kilograms). They spend more time on their own, grazing and playing with other yearlings. Their mothers have given birth to new calves, which need lots of attention and care.

The young bison continue to grow for three or four more years, until they become adults. Then the males go off on their own, or join other young bulls in a bachelor group. The females usually stay in their mother's band.

They will roam the plains, find mates, and raise calves of their own. And the herds will grow larger and larger. Maybe one day, they will again reach as far as the eye can see.

Bison
FUNFACT:

In the early 1800s, there were at least 30 million and maybe as many as 200 million bison in North America.

My PRAIRIE ANIMALS Adventures

The date of my adventure: _____

The people who came with me: _____

_____

Where I went: _____

What prairie animals I saw:

_____   _____

_____   _____

_____   _____

_____   _____

The date of my adventure: _____

The people who came with me: _____

_____

Where I went: _____

What prairie animals I saw:

_____   _____

_____   _____

_____   _____

_____   _____

My PRAIRIE ANIMALS Adventures

The date of my adventure: _____

The people who came with me: _____

_____

Where I went: _____

What prairie animals I saw:

_____   _____

_____   _____

_____   _____

_____   _____

The date of my adventure: _____

The people who came with me: _____

_____

Where I went: _____

What prairie animals I saw:

_____   _____

_____   _____

_____   _____

_____   _____

Explore the Fascinating World of . . .

HAWKS

Wayne Lynch
Illustrations by Fred Smith

HAWKS LIVE IN surprising ways. In the burning heat of the Arizona desert, Harris's hawks hunt like wolves in packs of four and five. In the cold Arctic, rough-legged hawks tear scraps of frozen meat from the bodies of seals killed by polar bears. In the dark spruce forests of Alaska and Canada, the northern goshawk (GOSS-hawk) attacks hares with the fierceness of a warrior. And in the prairies every autumn, the powerful Swainson's hawk leaves the big skies and soars south for two months to reach the center of South America, a distance of 6,000 miles (9,654 km). There, the Swainson's hawks spend the winter eating grasshoppers, with anteaters and armadillos as their neighbors. Then in the spring, the hawks circle and soar their way back to North America, where they live all summer with badgers and white-tailed deer. Here, the hawks hunt ground squirrels, ground squirrels, and more ground squirrels.

In autumn, most red-tailed hawks leave Alaska and Canada and migrate to the central and southern United States for the winter.

The largest feathers on a redtail are at the tip of the bird's wings. Biologists call these large feathers primaries.

Hawks are called birds of prey (PRAY), or raptors (RAP-torz). They hunt and eat other animals, or prey, for their living. A hawk's most important features are its head, feet, and wings.

To begin with, a hawk's eyes are very big. The coffee-colored eyes of a red-tailed hawk are almost as large as those of an adult human, even though the human is 50 times heavier than the hawk. A hawk's large eyes are very sensitive to details, so these birds see much better than a human does. For example, if a hawk and a human stood at one end of a football field, the hawk could easily see a grasshopper hop across the goal line at the other end of the field. The poor-sighted human would have to walk more than half the length of the field before he could hope to see the grasshopper leap for the touchdown.

Hawks
FUNFACT:

Hawks live all over North America, from the High Arctic tundra of Canada to the prairies, mountains, forests, and deserts of the United States. One of the best places to watch hawks is on the prairies, where there are no trees to hide them from view.

The following popular hawk-watching areas are indicated by the numbers above. The arrows show the hawks' autumn migration routes.

1. Hawk Mountain, Pennsylvania
2. Cape May, New Jersey
3. Holiday Beach, Ontario
4. Hawk Ridge, Minnesota
5. Coastal Bend, Texas
6. Manzano Mountains, New Mexico
7. Goshute Mountains, Nevada
8. Golden Gate, California
9. Cardel, Veracruz, Mexico

The ferruginous hawk, like all hawks, has a bony ridge above its eyes,
which gives the bird a fierce appearance.

In many hawks, the color of their eyes changes as they get older. When woodland hawks such as the northern goshawk, Cooper's hawk, and sharp-shinned hawk hatch they have gray eyes. At one year old, their eyes are yellow or orange. A year or two after that, they change to darker shades of red. Eye color does not affect how well a hawk sees, but it does tell its companions how old it is. In this way, a female hawk searching for an older, more experienced male partner only needs to check the color of his eyes to see if he would make a good father for her chicks.

Hawks have a third eyelid, called the nictitating (NICK-ti-tay-ting) membrane, that protects their large, sensitive eyes. This glassy-looking membrane sweeps over the eye from the inside corner and protects it in dangerous situations where the eye might be accidentally injured. This might happen when hawks fight with each other, when they feed their chicks beak-to-beak, or when they fly through shrubs or branches to chase a rabbit or bird.

Hawks
FUNFACT:

The smallest hawk in North America is the sharp-shinned hawk. It's about the size of a blue jay. The largest is the ferruginous hawk of the prairies. The ferruginous hawk is more than 10 times heavier than the sharp-shinned, and has a wingspan of 56 inches (142 cm), nearly the height of an average adult man.

The small beak on a rough-legged hawk matches the small size of its common prey, the lemming. Hawks with larger beaks are able to cut and tear apart the tough skin of larger prey.

Most hawks use their excellent vision to find and catch their prey. It is different for most owls, which hunt at night and rely on their sharp hearing to help them. One hawk, the northern harrier (HAIR-ee-er), is a daytime hawk that often hunts like a nighttime owl. The harrier has a round face, just like an owl. The harrier also has sensitive ears, which it uses to locate mice and similar rodents called voles hidden under shrubs and grass. When it is windy, the harrier can no longer hear the faint rustles of rodents running under the grass. Then it must use its eyes to hunt like other hawks.

Hawks
FUNFACT:

Most male and female hawks have similar coloring. The northern harrier is different. The male is gray and white, and the female is brown.

The long legs of the northern harrier help the bird to reach voles and mice hidden in thick grass.

Hawks have beaks like butcher knives that they use to slice their meals into bite-sized pieces. A hawk's beak grows all its life and always stays sharp from regular use. In zoos, hawks are sometimes fed foods that are too soft for them, so their beaks do not wear down as much as they do in the wild. If the beak grows too much, the hawk cannot eat properly. When this happens, a zookeeper must file off the extra growth on the bird's beak before it can eat normally again.

The fearsome feet of a hawk are its best weapon in making a kill. Three toes face forward and a fourth toe faces backward. Each toe on a hawk's foot ends with a long, sharp claw, called a talon (TAL-un). The fourth toe usually has the longest talon. When a hawk grabs an unlucky victim, it is often this long talon that kills the prey. Hawks have a powerful grip, and they squeeze their prey over and over again until it dies. Hawks with the largest feet and strongest talons hunt the biggest prey, such as rabbits and ground squirrels. Bird-hunting hawks, such as the sharp-shinned hawk and Cooper's hawk, are smaller, but they have especially long toes and talons. This helps them to penetrate, or pierce through, the fluffy feathers that cover their prey.

Hawks
FUNFACT:

Female hawks are larger and stronger than the males. The size difference is greatest in the accipiters. For example, the female sharp-shinned hawk weighs almost twice as much as the male.

After a summer thunderstorm, a juvenile Swainson's hawk spreads its wings to dry its feathers in the sunshine.

The broad tail and wings of this red-tailed hawk identify it as a buteo.

The shape of a hawk's wings and tail tells a lot about where the bird lives. Hawks that hunt mostly in open country such as prairies, arctic tundra, meadows, fields, and marshes usually have long, wide wings and a short, broad tail. Their large wings and tail help them to circle and soar higher and higher into the sky without having to flap and do much work. Twelve of the 16 species (SPEE-sees), or kinds, of hawks that live in the United States and Canada are built like this. Scientists call them buteos (BEWT-ee-ohs), or soaring hawks.

The northern goshawk fans its long tail to slow its speed before it lands.

Three other species of hawks live and hunt in thick forests where there are tree trunks and branches that can interfere with flying. These hawks, which scientists call accipiters (ack-SIP-ih-turs), have short, rounded wings and a long tail. When they fly, they usually do not soar. Instead, they flap and glide through the trees. Their short wings allow them to pick up speed quickly, and their long tail helps them to swerve and change directions rapidly, something the soaring hawks cannot do.

63

Only the northern harrier has bright white rump feathers, which is an easy way to identify this hawk.

One other hawk, the northern harrier, has a different shape from all the rest and belongs in a group by itself. Harriers have long, narrow wings and a long tail. The long wings and tail help it to fly slowly and quietly, close to the ground, so it can listen for prey. It frequently hunts in meadows and marshes, where there are no trees to avoid, so it does not need the ability to dodge and swerve quickly like an accipiter.

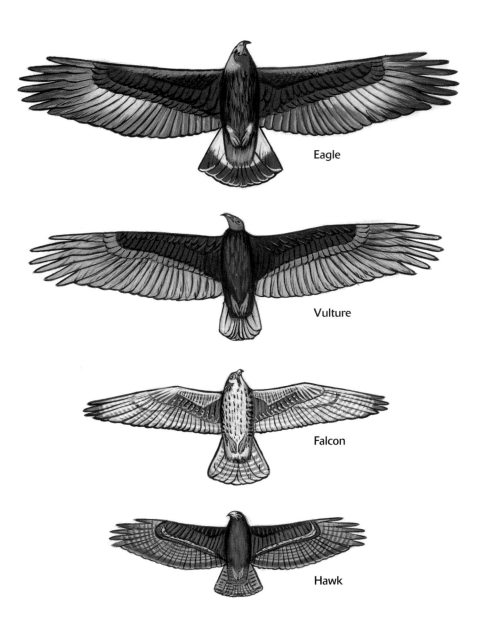

Eagle

Vulture

Falcon

Hawk

The shape of a raptor's wings and tail differ
depending upon whether it soars, flaps, or dives.

A bold male red-winged blackbird chases away a female northern harrier that flew too close to its nest.

Hawks, like most birds of prey, are meat eaters, but what they eat depends on where they live. Rough-legged hawks in the Arctic mostly eat small rodents called lemmings. Red-tailed hawks in central Washington munch on different kinds of snakes, while red-tails in Utah hunt jackrabbits. Red-shouldered hawks in Michigan eat crayfish, frogs, and toads. Cooper's hawks in the prairies chase robins, doves, and sparrows. Throughout most of the prairies, Swainson's hawks eat ground squirrels, but on the Oklahoma prairies some of these hawks hunt bats as they pour out of their caves at nightfall to search for insects.

Hawks hunt in different ways. The soaring hawks, or buteos, often hunt while flying. They circle high in the sky, watching for a careless animal that might become their next meal. When they spot a target, they quickly drop out of the sky and swoop in for the kill. If they can, they hide their final approach by flying behind a hill or some trees or shrubs. Then they attack by surprise. Even though the soaring hawks are masters of flight, they hunt more often by standing still. First they find an elevated perch such as a tree branch, a telephone pole, or the edge of a cliff. Then they stand and stare. When something flutters, runs, or wiggles, the sharp-eyed hawk dives with a foot full of talons.

Hawks
FUNFACT:

Small songbirds, crows, and jays will often mob a hawk that is perched nearby to drive it away. The birds swoop around the hawk in groups and call noisily to attract attention. Red-winged blackbirds and kingbirds are bold enough to actually attack a hawk and peck it.

The northern goshawk commonly hunts ruffed grouse, especially male grouse, which are less careful during the spring breeding season.

The forest-hunting accipiters are sneaky hunters. Often they hide among the branches of a tree. Then when a songbird passes nearby, they explode from their hiding place with lightning speed, and grab the victim in a puff of feathers. If the songbird swerves and flees, the chase is on. The hunter and the hunted zigzag through the forest in a race almost too fast to follow. Most times, the songbird wins the race and the hungry hawk goes back to hide and sneak again.

When a red-tailed hawk makes a kill, it often moves the prey to an elevated perch where it is safer to eat.

Harriers and some buteos, especially the rough-legged hawk, hunt by flying slowly, back and forth, close to the ground. Mice and voles can only see things close up, so hawks that hunt like this are invisible to their prey. When the searching hawk hears a squeak or sees the grass move, it may hover for a moment to pinpoint the target. Then, with its feet outstretched, it drops like a rock and snatches the mouse. Often, though, the hawk misses and the mouse lives to squeak another day.

White-tailed hawks commonly hunt animals as they flee from the flames of prairie grass fires.

Even though hawks are skillful hunters, they often go hungry. They must use every trick they know to catch a meal. Two southern hawks have an unusual way of catching prey. In Texas, the white-tailed hawks watch for prairie fires, and as many as 60 hawks may fly in for dinner. The fire-loving hawks hover in the choking smoke or drift back and forth in front of the flames, gobbling up lizards, snakes, insects, and rodents fleeing for their lives. Behind the flames, other hawks search the burned grasses for critters that did not survive.

Texas and Arizona are home to another hawk with a surprising way to hunt. The Harris's hawk of the desert hunts in packs, something that no other hawk in the world is known to do. Packs of five hawks are the most common, and the birds are always related to each other. Usually one or both parents and their young join together. Their favorite prey are desert cottontails, ground squirrels, and wood rats. The birds chase their prey in relay races to tire it out, or they surprise it by attacking from different directions at once. Another trick is for one or two birds to chase the prey on foot and flush it into the open, where it is attacked by another hawk that was perched and waiting.

Hawks
FUNFACT:

The most common hawk in North America is the red-tailed hawk. It lives everywhere from the arctic tree line to Mexico.

Three fledgling Harris's hawks perch on a cactus, waiting for their parents to feed them. A fledgling is a young bird that has left the nest.

Some hawk prey fight back. Many red-tailed hawks have scars on their legs from sharp-toothed mammals such as rabbits, hares, and squirrels. One scientist saw a red-tailed hawk attack a weasel and try to fly away with it, but the angry weasel bit and killed the hawk in self defense.

Another animal that may fight back is a rattlesnake, and rattlesnake venom can kill a hawk. Even so, different hawks try their luck with the deadly snakes, and the hawk usually wins. The snake strikes the bird in the body or wings and gets nothing but a mouth full of feathers. The hawk then kills the snake by pecking it on the head.

One kind of animal that never fights back is a dead one. Hawks that live on the prairies and in the Arctic seem especially good at finding dead animals, called carrion (CARE-ee-un). It may be the lack of trees that makes the carcasses (KAR-kus-iz), or dead bodies, easier to locate. Red-tailed hawks, Swainson's hawks, rough-legged hawks, and northern harriers all eat carrion.

Winter can be one of the biggest killers of wildlife, and many hawks eat carrion in early spring when live prey may be scarce, or hard to find. Another wildlife killer is the automobile, and many hawks eat the flattened carcasses on the roadways. Sometimes these feasting hawks stuff themselves so full they cannot fly away quickly enough and are killed by other vehicles that drive by.

If a hawk cannot catch its own food, or find some that is already dead, it can always become a pirate and steal from others. This is common among hawks. The red-tailed hawk is large and powerful, and it steals meals from rough-legged hawks, northern harriers, peregrine (PER-uh-gren) falcons, and prairie falcons. The harriers and short-eared owls often steal from each other.

A snow goose is too large for a harrier to kill.
This goose was already dead when the harrier found it.

Adult Swainson's hawks scream loudly whenever a predator approaches their nest.

Hawks may use calls to try to scare away others stealing their food or invading their territory. They use their calls for many other reasons, too. Hawks call to search for a mate, or they yell to brag that they own a piece of prairie or patch of forest and that they will defend it from outsiders.

Different hawks have different calls. Some scream and whistle, and others squeak or bark, sometimes from a perch, sometimes from the ground, and sometimes from high in the sky. The steam-whistle scream of the red-tailed hawk is the most familiar call of any hawk in North America, because the cry of this hawk has been used in many movies and on television.

Hawks are noisiest during the spring when it is time to raise a family.

When hawks are ready to mate, the first thing they do is to scream to let others know. Partners often call together, circle and soar together, and sky dance. In sky dancing, the male, and sometimes the female, swoops up and down across the sky in the pattern of a giant roller coaster. Other times, the male flies above his partner and then dives toward her. Just before they collide, the female flips upside down and the two birds briefly touch talons, like friends holding hands.

Many hawks have the same partner for several years, and some may mate for life. Others, such as the northern harrier, have a different partner every spring. Some male harriers may have seven female partners during a single mating season!

The red-shouldered hawk lives in woodlands where its call may be heard even though the bird may stay hidden.

The parents of these Swainson's hawk eggs used fresh aspen twigs and leaves to build their nest.

All hawks build nests. The most common place is in a tree. In places where there are no trees, the birds nest on cliffs or on the ground. A pair of hawks may repair an old nest from a past season or build a new one. Usually, both the male and the female gather twigs, bark, and grass for the nest, but the female does all the building.

A hundred and fifty years ago on the prairies, ferruginous (feh-ROO-juh-nus) hawks sometimes built nests using old bison ribs and lined the nest with the wool from these shaggy beasts. Today, with many bison gone, the hawks use sticks and chips of dried cattle dung.

One of the most interesting habits of nesting hawks is their use of green leaves and twigs in building their nests. Often, they start doing this before they even lay eggs. Many pairs continue to add fresh greenery until the chicks are quite large. The most likely reason they do this is to prevent flies, ticks, and fleas from settling in the nest. These pests feed on bird blood and that is harmful to small, helpless chicks. Green plants such as pine needles and the leaves and twigs of cottonwood trees help to protect the chicks because they produce strong smelling chemicals that insects do not like.

Hawks
FUNFACT:

Hawk droppings would quickly dirty their nests if they were not careful. From an early age, chicks always point their bottoms over the edge of the nest when they poop.

Most hawks lay just two to four eggs each year. That is not many when you consider that a gray partridge lays 15 eggs, and a domestic chicken may lay over 300 in a year. Once a female hawk starts to lay her eggs, the male hawk does all the hunting for himself and his partner. In fact, the male hawk may start feeding his mate several weeks before she begins laying. He continues to feed her like a princess for the whole month while she sits on her eggs and warms them. This period is called incubation (ink-you-BAY-shun). Even after the chicks hatch, the male hawk hunts for his entire family until the young are about half grown. A male harrier may catch 40 voles a day to feed his family. One scientist observed a male broad-winged hawk that brought 11 voles, 8 snakes, 5 frogs, and 3 birds to his nest in just three days, and there was only one chick to feed.

Growing chicks have big appetites. After a few weeks, the male hawk cannot hunt fast enough to keep his partner and his chicks filled with food, so the female hawk must start to hunt for the family as well.

Hawks
FUNFACT:

Large hawks live longer than small ones. The red-tailed hawk and ferruginous hawk may live 15 to 20 years, whereas the small sharp-shinned and Cooper's hawks rarely live more than 4 or 5 years.

A female sharp-shinned hawk will brood her chicks, or sit on them to keep them warm, for about 10 days.

This rough-legged hawk chick used the white egg tooth on the tip of its beak to free itself from the eggshell.

Usually a hawk's eggs do not hatch at the same time. As a result, the chicks are different ages and sizes. Naturally, the largest chicks are able to beg the loudest and so are fed first, while the smaller ones get shoved out of the way. When there is a lot of food this is not a problem. The smaller chicks simply wait until their larger nest mates are full, and then they can eat. When prey is scarce, however, it is a different story. The largest chicks hog all the food, and the smaller chicks go hungry and may even starve. In Swainson's hawks and rough-legged hawks, the largest chicks may even attack their smaller brothers and sisters and peck them to death. The parents never try to stop these deadly food fights.

When a chick starves or is killed, it also may be eaten. The mother hawk may tear it up and feed it to her other

This female northern harrier feeds her chick small bits of meat until it is strong enough to feed itself.

chicks or she may eat it herself. When food is scarce, nothing is wasted.

Although the adult male hawk does the hunting for the family, only the female feeds the chicks. Usually when a male returns with food he screams to his mate. He may stop at a special perch nearby, called a plucking post. The plucking post is usually an old nest, a log on the forest floor, or a large limb on a tree. Here the male prepares the prey for his family. If the meal is a songbird or small mammal, he usually cuts off the head and eats that himself. Then he plucks out some of the feathers or fur and removes and eats the insides. Dinner is now ready to be served. The female hawk flies over and collects the meal, or the male delivers it directly to her at the nest. The male hawk never stays around for dinner, and the female always feeds the chicks alone.

Young Cooper's hawks spend a month in the nest after which they hop to branches nearby.

At first, when the chicks are still balls of white fuzz, they are fed tiny bits of meat. As they get older, the bits get bigger. By the time they are three or four weeks old the chicks can feed themselves. The hungry chicks squabble and steal from each other. They guard their meals by spreading their wings over the food to hide it from the others. This guarding behavior, called mantling (MANT-ling), is something a young hawk will do for the rest of its life whenever it catches a meal and wants to hide it from other hawks.

At this stage in the nesting cycle, the parents will fiercely defend their young and often attack animals that might be a threat. They have spent several months of hard work raising their family and they want the chicks to survive. If a predator (PRED-uh-tor), such as a great horned owl or coyote, comes near the nest, the adults may attack. They may also attack other hawks, eagles, or wildlife photographers that get too close. A ferruginous hawk will attack a red fox half a mile from its nest and strike the animal so hard that it knocks it over. The taloned feet of an angry northern goshawk can strike at 50 miles per hour (80 kph). Such a blow can seriously injure even an animal as big as a black bear that is foolish enough to climb up to the bird's nest. Few bears are so brave or so hungry.

Hawks
FUNFACT:

Hawks are not brightly colored. Most are brown, black, or gray on top and pale with streaks underneath.

The prairie Swainson's hawk is especially fierce in defending its nest and young. The male patrols from high in the sky and dives on any trespassers. They try to rake their enemies with their sharp talons to drive them away. Even crows and harmless turkey vultures (VULL-churz) may be attacked. If the trespasser is another Swainson's hawk the two birds may lock talons in a midair battle, and spiral, or twist, through the air. Most of the time, the fighters separate and neither is injured. Sometimes, however, the hawks get badly cut, break a wing, or even die if they crash into the ground.

Hawks
FUNFACT:

At the base of every hawk's beak is a bright yellow fleshy area called the cere (SEAR). There are no feathers on the cere and this may help the hawk keep its face clean and free of blood when it feeds on fresh prey.

The necks on these young Swainson's hawk chicks are swollen because they have just been fed by their mother.

Snakes, including venomous rattlesnakes, are a common food in the diet of the red-tailed hawk.

At four to six weeks of age, most hawk chicks are ready to leave home. They usually cannot fly well yet, but they can flutter, hop, and jump, and that is what they do. They jump out of the nest and hop along nearby branches. Scientists call these young hawks "branchers." For the next month or two, the hawk parents will continue to feed their chicks as they become stronger and better flyers. At first, the chicks will return to the nest during the day to be fed, and at night to sleep. Eventually, though, the whole family moves away from the nest and none return.

A young fledgling ferruginous hawk on the ground will defend itself with its strong feet and sharp talons.

Adult hawks do not teach their chicks to hunt. The chicks must learn on their own. At first, the young hawks will chase each other, attack sticks and clumps of mud, and practice diving and landing. Many young hawks will jump about in the grass to catch crickets, grasshoppers, lizards, and small snakes. Some will steal food from their nest mates, their parents, or other adults. Carrion may also be important to young hawks still learning to hunt.

The most difficult time in a young hawk's life is the first weeks and months after its parents stop the free meals. This is when they must hunt or starve. In good years, only half the young hawks die. In bad years, most will die before they are one year old. A lack of food kills most of them, but some die in crashes with automobiles or power lines. Others are killed by larger hawks or by great horned owls, one of the most powerful raptors in North America.

A northern goshawk mantles over a freshly killed ruffed grouse. This behavior hides the dead bird from thieves such as ravens and other goshawks.

The Harris's hawk, which lives in deserts, does not need to migrate in winter and lives in its territory year-round.

When deep snow covers the ground, it is difficult for a hawk to find food. Because of this, most of the hawks that live in the arctic tundra and the northern forests of Canada and Alaska migrate in winter. Most fly south to the United States and Mexico where the winters are warmer. Some, such as the broad-winged hawk and Swainson's hawk, are long-distance travelers and journey all the way to South America. Both soar in great flocks for several months to reach their wintering grounds.

In the autumn, a bird-watcher may see a thousand of these hawks soaring overhead in a single day as they fly south, an event that thrills more and more people every year. Hawk watching was not always such a popular pastime. Just a hundred years ago, hawks were poisoned and shot as pests. Rewards were paid for their severed, or cut off, feet. People thought hawks were mean, bloodthirsty beasts, and that the only good hawk was a dead hawk. Today, people think differently. All hawks are protected. They are an important part of a healthy wild world and they need protection so that future children can enjoy these magnificent birds of prey.

My PRAIRIE ANIMALS Adventures

The date of my adventure: _____

The people who came with me: _____

_____

Where I went: _____

What prairie animals I saw:

_____   _____

_____   _____

_____   _____

_____   _____

The date of my adventure: _____

The people who came with me: _____

_____

Where I went: _____

What prairie animals I saw:

_____   _____

_____   _____

_____   _____

My PRAIRIE ANIMALS Adventures

The date of my adventure: _____

The people who came with me: _____

_____

Where I went: _____

What prairie animals I saw:

_____   _____

_____   _____

_____   _____

_____   _____

The date of my adventure: _____

The people who came with me: _____

_____

Where I went: _____

What prairie animals I saw:

_____   _____

_____   _____

_____   _____

_____   _____

Explore the Fascinating World of . . .

PRAIRIE DOGS

Marybeth Lorbiecki
Illustrations by Wayne Ford

THE BUSIEST PLACE for wildlife on a prairie is a prairie dog town. With burrows below and mounds above, these towns are bursting with activity. Prairie dogs are jumping, digging, wrestling, yipping, grooming, cleaning, kissing, and chasing. Their high-pitched calls and chirps ring out over the grasses.

Eagles soar overhead, and coyotes patrol. They both wait to catch a prairie dog unprepared. Bison and cattle take dust baths in the dirt mounds around the town's holes. On other mounds, burrowing owls line up and watch the action. Underground, in the prairie dogs' abandoned tunnels, snakes, spiders, salamanders, box turtles, rabbits, and mice slither and scurry. Without prairie dogs, many of these animals would be without homes and food.

Prairie dogs are extremely smart. They watch everything, have excellent memories, and chat to each other about what they see.

Prairie dog towns attract many other animals. Bison, cattle, and antelope like to graze near them.

Prairie dogs may bark, yip, and snarl, but they are not dogs. They are ground squirrels. Their ears and tails are shorter than most squirrels' and their claws are longer. Even so, prairie dogs are related to the nut-grabbing neighbors found in backyards. Prairie dogs are also related to chipmunks, woodchucks, and marmots.

With small rounded heads and ears nearly hidden in fur, prairie dogs can slip into narrow holes and winding tunnels easily. From head to tail, most prairie dogs measure from 11 to 13 inches (28 to 33 cm). The tail reaches out another 3 to 4 inches (8 to 10 cm). They have short legs, but they can run up to 35 miles (56 km) per hour for short sprints.

Prairie Dog
FUNFACT:

Prairie dogs have been called "sod poodles," "barking squirrels," "prairie rats," and *petits chiens*," or little dogs. Their scientific name, *Cynomys*, means mouse-dog squirrel.

Prairie dogs rarely go more than 30 feet (less than 10 meters) from their burrows.
That is only about the length of five adult men lined up foot to head.

This black-tailed prairie dog has fattened up for winter, when food is scarce. It will lose as much as half its body weight before spring.

In the winter and spring, prairie dogs are as slender as minks. But once the grasses start sprouting, prairie dogs spend a great deal of time eating. Through the summer and fall, they grow fatter and fatter, until their roly-poly bodies ripple as they run. The prairie dogs need this extra weight. They have to live most of the winter on their fat.

Adult prairie dogs range in weight from 1.5 to 3 pounds (.7 to 1.4 kg). They range in color from golden or reddish brown to gray, with darker ears and lighter colored bellies and snouts. Some prairie dogs look black when they have been digging in soil with coal dust, but there are no truly black prairie dogs. However, there are some rare white prairie dogs.

Prairie dogs live in Mexico, the United States, and Canada, in the dry grassy areas of the western plains and Rocky Mountain foothills. There are five different kinds, or species (SPEE-sees).

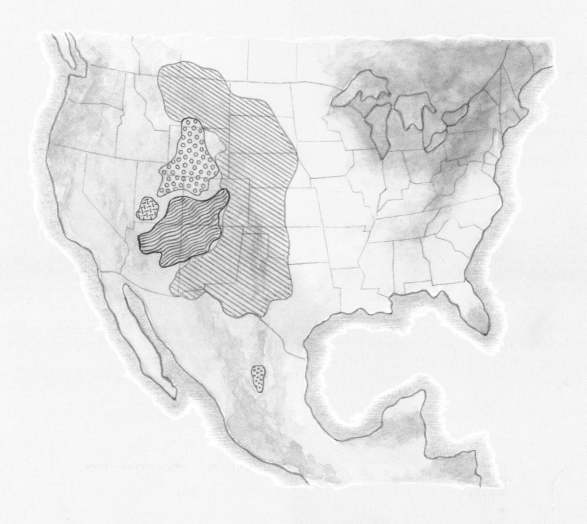

 Black-tailed

 Gunnison's

 White-tailed

 Mexican

 Utah

White-tailed prairie dogs are found in the foothills and mountain meadows of the Rockies.

The prairie dogs that like the high deserts and mountain valleys have white-tipped tails. These species are the white-tailed prairie dog, the Gunnison's prairie dog, and the Utah prairie dog. Since they live in higher places with colder temperatures, they tend to hibernate, or sleep through the harsh winters.

The white-tailed prairie dog is the most common of the high-ground species. It can be found in a few mountain meadows of Colorado, Utah, Wyoming, and Montana. It is less talkative and social than its cousins.

Prairie Dog
FUNFACT:

Grazing animals, such as cattle, bison, and antelope, like to eat near prairie dog towns. The grasses and flowers have greater nutrition and likely taste better. The grazers also use the prairie dog mounds for dirt baths to get rid of pesky insects.

Gunnison's prairie dogs do not dig as deep as some of the other species. Their tunnels are only about 3.5 feet (1 m) deep.

The Gunnison's prairie dog has a darker body and a shorter tail than most of the other prairie dogs. The Gunnison's prairie dog can be seen in the high, dry plains of the Four Corners area. This is where New Mexico, Colorado, Arizona, and Utah meet. These dogs are more like ground squirrels than other prairie dogs. They live in smaller groups and build smaller mounds.

The Utah prairie dog is the least common of all the high-ground prairie dogs. It is easy to tell from the other species because it is the smallest and has a spot of black above the eyes. It lives in just a few places in the mountain valleys of central Utah.

The prairie dog species that live on the low, dry grasslands have black-tipped tails and do not hibernate. They are the black-tailed prairie dog and the Mexican prairie dog.

The black-tailed prairie dog is the largest and most numerous of all prairie dog species. It can be found in small patches of grasslands and prairies in Canada down through the western plains of the United States to Mexico.

Prairie Dog
FUNFACT:

Prairie dogs help prairies grow. By eating weedy plants, they keep prairie grasses and flowers from being choked out. They churn up the soil when they tunnel, loosening the soil for roots, air, and water. The prairie dogs also add fertilizer with their leavings.

The Utah prairie dog is rare. It was placed on the Endangered Species List in 1973. It is only found in five counties of southwest Utah, high in the mountains.

When looking for food, male prairie dogs wander a bit farther from the burrow than females. This black-tailed prairie dog is enjoying a sunflower.

Though the black-tailed prairie dog is the most numerous of all the species, it is not common. Once, prairie dogs were seen all across the Great Plains of North America, along with the bison. Prairie dogs used to number in the hundreds of millions. But, like the bison, they are now only found in small areas far from each other. One particular kind of black-tailed prairie dog, the Arizona prairie dog, has died out completely. It is extinct (ex-TINKD).

The Mexican prairie dog, the other species from non-mountain areas, is extremely rare. It lives in only a few places in Mexico.

Prairie dogs are named after North America's natural grasslands. These prairies are filled with many different kinds of wild grasses and flowers, which is why prairie dogs do so well there. They are mostly vegetarians, or plant eaters. They feast on shoots, seeds, stalks, and flowers. Though they are named after the prairie, these animals are not found only in prairies. The black-tailed prairie dog can sometimes live in fields or meadows of other grasses as long as they can crop the plants short with their teeth.

The dinner of choice for prairie dogs depends on the season and what plants are growing. In times of heavy snow or during drought (DROWT), when grasses die, prairie dogs dig out and nibble roots. The dogs that live in more desert-like spaces eat prickly pear and other cactus. They also gnaw (NAW) on bushes and small trees, such as sagebrush and mesquite (mes-KEET) trees. Prairie dogs, except the white-tailed species, chew up weedy plants, too, including dandelions and thistles (THISS-uls).

Prairie Dog
FUNFACT:

Scientists estimate that it takes about 429 prairie dogs to eat the amount of grass one cow eats in a day. An adult prairie dog eats about 25 pounds (11.4 kg) of grass per year.

Members of a coterie work and talk together for protection.
These four white-tailed prairie dogs stand alert and keep watch.

Prairie dogs use their long claws for tugging up grasses and picking up food, tunneling, grooming, and defending themselves.

Prairie dogs occasionally feed on grasshoppers or other insects. They are able to pick up small things easily because they have finger-like separations to their paws, like raccoons. So they can grasp a clump of grass or pick up a beetle.

Prairie dogs have tall front teeth, like other rodents. They can tear off a bunch of tough grasses with little effort. Then the back molars start to work, grinding these plants to a pulp. Prairie dogs have 22 teeth in all.

To wash their food down, prairie dogs only have their own saliva. They don't need to drink! Their bodies make water from some foods they eat, and they swallow dew with the plants they chew in the early mornings. There is also some water in the plants and insects they eat.

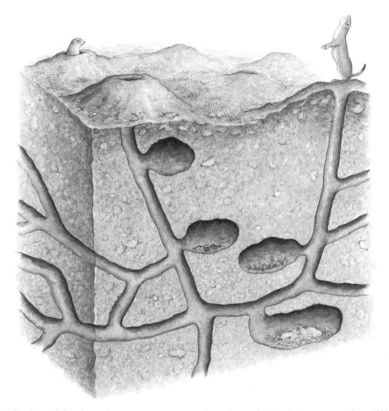

Black-tailed prairie dogs have numerous chambers in their burrows for different functions: nesting, sleeping, food storage, and others. A single tunnel can extend as far as 100 feet (about 30 m) or one-third the size of a football field.

Prairie dogs are champion diggers. They use their long claws to tunnel out group homes deep underground. The burrows of black-tailed prairie dogs usually go down at a steep slant for 12 to 15 feet (3.7 to 4.6 m). Then they flatten and spread out in long tunnels leading 20 to 50 feet (6.1 to 15.3 m) farther to escape exits. There are chambers built along the way, with rooms for storing food, birthing and nursing young, hiding, sleeping, and other uses.

In hard, dry, clay-like soils, prairie dog tunnels do not go down as deep. The digging is just too much work!

Prairie dogs are the most clannish members of the squirrel family. They live in large groups called coteries (KO-tir-ees). A black-tailed prairie dog coterie usually includes one adult male, three or four adult females, and their young. These coteries often live right next to other coteries, like neighborhoods in a prairie dog town. The burrows of each coterie, though, are not connected.

Prairie dogs are feisty toward strangers, and they strongly defend their territories.

Prairie dogs have keen senses of smell and hearing, which help them avoid tunneling into each other's burrows. Should they do so, there would be trouble. The winner of the fight would then chase off the intruder and block the tunnel.

Prairie Dog
FUNFACT:

One prairie dog town in Texas reached 250 miles (402 km) in one direction and 100 miles (161 km) in another. It was estimated that 400 million prairie dogs lived there!

These young black-tailed pups practice being protective adults and defending their ground by rough play.

In a prairie dog town, there are usually 5 to 35 adult prairie dogs for every acre (.4 ha). A single burrow has from one to six openings. The average town ends up with more than 50 holes per acre. Not all of these are being used. Some are abandoned because predators (PRED-uh-torz) or illness killed off too many members of the coterie, or there was not enough food.

A larger town can get sectioned off into smaller parts, too. This happens if some part of the landscape splits the town, such as a river or a rocky ridge.

These young black-tailed prairie dogs are getting their first look at the outside world.

Each species of prairie dog makes the kinds of burrow entrances and exits that work best for their dirt and landscape. Black-tailed prairie dogs make three different kinds.

The first type of hole has a mound around it that looks like a little volcano. This is a major entrance, and the dogs take a great deal of time building and rebuilding the mound. They form the shape with their paws and tamp, or pack, the dirt with their foreheads. These mounds can be as tall as 3 feet (.9 m). The opening is only 6 to 12 inches (15 to 30 cm) across. It gets even narrower underground and is only 3 to 4 inches (8 to 10 cm) wide. The hole is big enough for prairie dogs, but not for coyotes!

A coterie may have more than one of these volcano mounds because they are so useful. Besides giving the dogs easy escape hatches into their homes, these volcano mounds work like watchtowers. Standing on top of the mound, the dogs get a good view in all directions of their grassy territory and the lands around it. The volcano mounds also keep rivers of rainwater from pouring down into the burrows. On hot, dry days, the mounds create an air-vent system. They draw fresh air through the tunnels to carry the heat away.

Prairie Dog
FUNFACT:

The most powerful male dog in the coterie, or the "top dog," gets the best place on the volcano mound and the first choice of grasses.

This black-tailed dog is on the run to get back to the burrow with its treasure before it gets caught!

Just underneath the opening of the volcano mound is an extra hollowed-out place big enough for a prairie dog to sit up. This is called the listening chamber. After a dog has spotted danger, such as a coyote, it will call out an alarm. Other dogs in the coterie and town will echo it and respond. The prairie dogs will all go on alert, facing the coyote, keeping their eyes on its every move.

Any dog that has strayed too far from its own holes will rush back. If it has to pop into another coterie's hole to escape the coyote, it could face danger there, too!

This time, despite these prairie dogs calling to each other, the coyote got one. Sometimes a coyote and a badger will work together to catch a dog for dinner.

If the coyote gets too close to one of the dogs on its watchtower, the dog will duck into the listening chamber to let its ears do the work. It will not pop up its head again until there is no sound of the predator or an all-clear call has been sounded by another prairie dog.

Once the coyote is seen leaving the area, one or more of the dogs watching it leave will yip the all-clear call. The other dogs will echo this. Soon all the dogs in hiding will come out and go back to their work of eating, grooming, cleaning, and mound building.

A black-tailed dog pops up from its escape hatch to see if all is safe.

The second kind of hole is a dirt hill, which is not carefully tended. It is made of all the loose dirt that came out of the tunnel when it was dug. The hills are only 4 to 5 inches (10 to 13 cm) tall, but they serve as perfect back doors.

Finally, there are escape hatches that are just holes in the ground without mounds, and sometimes without connections to tunnels. These holes are often in the sides of hills or ditches. The prairie dogs duck in them to rest, take a break from the hot summer sun, or hide.

What are the prairie dogs hiding from?

Prairie Dog
FUNFACT:

Over 500 pounds (227 kg) of dirt are tossed out to make the average burrow.

Besides coyotes, prairie dogs stay on the alert for golden eagles, red-tailed hawks, and ferruginous (feh-ROO-juh-nus) hawks flying above them. The birds can swoop down and snatch the dogs from overhead. They are so dangerous that black-tailed prairie dogs have a special alarm call just for eagles and hawks. This is a jump-yip leap backwards in the air with two fast, high-pitched notes. At that signal, everyone nearby hits the tunnels. No one waits around to watch as they do with predators on the ground.

At night, black-footed ferrets stalk the dogs. Ferrets are slim enough to travel into the burrows. They live almost entirely off of eating prairie dogs.

Badgers are also a common predator. They are such fast diggers that they can go right after a prairie dog into its tunnel. Other predators are swift foxes, weasels, bobcats, ravens, wolves, rattlesnakes, pet or stray dogs, and humans.

Prairie Dog
FUNFACT:

Besides humans, prairie dogs have the most complex language system of any animals studied by scientists. Scientists use computers to recognize the different sound bits or "words." It seems prairie dogs even have grammar rules to their language!

Scientists are fascinated by the language of prairie dogs. The dogs communicate
not only to tell each other of danger, but for other reasons as well.

Prairie dogs protect themselves against predators by communicating with each other and working together. They are the most talkative members of the squirrel family. Their language system is amazing. Prairie dogs make many different sounds that they arrange in different ways for different messages. They also make their voices go high or low, fast or slow, and friendly or harsh to communicate different meanings.

Prairie dogs will scream when they are afraid, snarl when they fight, churr or buzz when they argue, and chirk or purr when they mate. Chirps are used to tell neighboring dogs where they are and to pass on other information. Scientists aren't sure what else is being said. Perhaps the dogs are commenting on the tastiness of certain grasses or when they should start their spring tunnel cleaning!

From far away, some of the calls

Prairie dogs mix actions with sounds to get attention and communicate. This jump-yip call alerts others to danger close by.

can sound like the baying of hounds. But up close, the bark of a prairie dog actually sounds more bird-like than dog-like, with a shrill *chee-chee-chee*. Each prairie dog species speaks a little differently. They have dialects (DY-a-lekts), or small differences in their calls. Gunnison's prairie dogs tend to have sharper, shorter calls than black-tailed prairie dogs. White-tailed prairie dogs are thought to have more musical tones. Even prairie dogs of the same species from different towns have slight differences in their calls.

Actions also tell a great deal. Tail flicking, jumping, bobbing, snarling, teeth chattering, and "kissing" all have meaning. When prairie dogs meet, they run up to each other, hug, and kiss. Scientists think they are actually rubbing their teeth together or checking scent glands. By taste and smell, a prairie dog can tell if another dog is a relative, friend, or enemy.

Prairie dogs greet each other by hugging and kissing. They also groom each other.

This black-tailed dog makes it clear that danger is still present.

Just like humans, prairie dogs use a combination of sounds and actions to communicate. Through careful studies and with the help of computers, scientists have discovered the meanings of some of their messages.

A jump-yip call means "Find cover!" The prairie dog closes its eyes and throws itself backward in the air while sending out a shrill "weee-oh!" sound. This urgent alarm is used by black-tailed prairie dogs to warn other dogs about eagles or hawks flying overhead, but it is not used by the species in the mountains. A bobbing bark, which has two short sounds repeated between quick bobs, means "Watch that predator." This bark often comes with a description of the predator. The all-clear whistle-like yip means "You can come out now." A snarled warning bark says "This is MY area. Stay out."

Prairie Dog
FUNFACT:

Prairie dogs describe details to each other. They will note the difference between colors of fur or clothing on an approaching intruder and whether they seem dangerous. They will even tell if a person has a gun!

These are just a few examples. The calls have individual pieces of sound that carry meaning, like words. The prairie dogs vary the words in the calls and their order to give more information. They will tell each other exactly what kind of predator is approaching, its speed, and even what it looks like, including its color and size. The dogs listening then take different actions according to which animal is on its way, from where, and how fast.

Prairie dogs also describe animals that are not a danger to them, such as antelope, deer, elk, and cows. Perhaps they do this much like newscasters give weather reports, simply to keep everyone updated on anything that might be moving, important, or surprising.

A prairie dog town is always an active place with kissing, chasing, grooming, eating, repairing mounds, cleaning out tunnels, and digging new ones. The dogs tend to rise and set with the sun. In the winter, most of the activity is underground. The high-ground prairie dogs completely hibernate during this time. The plains species simply spend less time above ground.

Prairie Dog
FUNFACT:

Prairie dogs "talk" about many things they see, even about harmless antelope and cattle that stroll by. Much of their language has yet to be decoded. Who knows what else they chat about!

Prairie dogs build up a thick fur for winter, which they shed in the spring.

When the snow covers the grasslands, prairie dogs have to dig to find food. They tend to eat far less, spending more time underground where it is warmer. They live off the fat they gained during the summer and fall.

As spring approaches, black-tailed prairie dogs start eating more and building their nests. This is a busy time. First they do some spring-cleaning, hauling out all the old, dirty grasses from the birthing chambers.

Then they drag fresh, new grasses in.

Spring is also mating time. Adult males are able to mate for only four to five weeks in spring. That's when they begin chirking their mating call, calling out their territories, and chasing any females within sight or sound.

Females are able to mate only four to five hours on a single spring day. So if they are not ready, they snarl and bite at any males that approach them.

Mother prairie dogs nurse their young for seven weeks.
They will protect the little ones against any enemies, even other prairie dog mothers.

When the females are ready to mate, they give their own chirking calls. Then every male that hears them makes a wild dash over. Sparring breaks out between the males to see who gets to mate first. Both males and females mate numerous times during this period.

After all the mating is over, the coteries settle down. The females, along with one top male, return to their home burrows. There are one to four females in each burrow. Each female has her own birthing and nursing chamber. In 34 to 35 days, the young are born. Usually, about three to five prairie dog pups are born in each chamber, but there can be as many as eight.

Dark red and wrinkled, the little pups are hairless and blind. Their eyes are shut tight. The mothers lick and rub them.

The pups are so small they fit in the palm of a child's hand. They are only 2.75 inches (7 cm) long. They weigh an average of half an ounce (14 g). That is about the weight of a few marbles.

The pups may start out tiny, but they grow fast. They drink milk from their mothers' bodies. In two weeks, they have more than doubled their size. By the fifth week, their eyes open.

However, only about half the young ever make it above ground to see sunlight. Sometimes a nursing prairie dog will attack and eat the young of another female in the burrow. It could be that the attacking mother has not had enough food to make milk and she is extremely hungry. Or she may need the other mother to help nurse her pups. Or there may not be much room to build new coteries in the area, and the attacking mother may want her pups to get the space that remains. Scientists do not know for sure what causes a mother to act this way.

Prairie Dog
FUNFACT:

Males and females mate with numerous partners. The young in any litter often have different fathers.

Young prairie dogs are called pups. They learn by watching, listening, and imitating.

Snakes, ferrets, and badgers also eat prairie dog pups. When these predators make their moves, prairie dog mothers fight to protect their pups. They will even gang up with other prairie dogs against a rattlesnake.

At six weeks old, all the pups that survive get their first look at the outside world. They play rough-and-tumble chasing games with the other pups. The adults check on the youngsters often, kissing and grooming them. When hungry, the pups come running to the closest adults to nurse. The males gently nudge them away. The females let them nurse, even if the pups are not their own young.

At seven weeks, the females also begin to nudge the pups away. Then the young must learn from the parents how to find plants and grasses to eat.

The adults have already begun teaching the pups about predators, using voice, tail, and body signals. Over the summer months, the young will begin answering back, imitating the adults.

By September, the young are almost as large as their parents, but they are not as fat or heavy. They scatter to make new homes in abandoned burrows or dig their own. Sometimes the parents will scatter instead and leave some of the young with the family burrow.

By the start of the second summer, the yearlings are about the same size as their parents. That fall, they will be fully grown. They may be ready to have young of their own the following spring, at about two years old. If food is scarce, or if other conditions are not right, they may not be ready to have young until the next spring.

Each fall and spring, the animals molt, or shed their old fur. In the spring, the new hair is thinner and shorter for the hot summer months. In the fall, it grows thicker and longer to warm them through the winter ahead.

Prairie Dog
FUNFACT:

Some of the largest prairie dog towns in the United States can be found on Native American reservations. The Cheyenne River Sioux have taken steps to protect prairie dogs and bison on their lands.

Prairie dogs in the wild live an average of four to five years. They do not grow larger with age. Some prairie dogs have been captured to live in zoos or as pets. They live an average of eight and a half years in captivity.

However, prairie dogs do not make good pets. They are great diggers, so no one's yard is safe. Also, their memories are too good! If a prairie dog feels scared or upset, or if someone mishandles a prairie dog, even by accident, the animal does not forget. It will snarl or bite or call out alarms whenever that person approaches, even if it is a month later.

In addition, captive prairie dogs can catch diseases from other animals. So even though they seem cute and friendly, it's a bad idea to capture or buy prairie dogs for pets.

This pup is looking for some attention. Both female and male adults in a coterie watch out for the young, though the females do most of the pup care.

Despite how smart and talkative prairie dogs are, their towns are shrinking and disappearing. Prairie dogs are found in less than two percent of the places they used to live. This is because most of their grassland habitats, or places for homes, have been used for ranching, farming, buildings, or roads.

Unfortunately, prairie dogs are not safe even in the national and state parks and grasslands. Government workers, ranchers, and farmers have been poisoning or shooting prairie dogs. They argue that prairie dogs eat up too much grass. They want the grass saved for cattle, sheep, and bison. They also fear that these animals will stumble in prairie dog holes and break their legs.

These are misunderstandings. Studies have shown over and over that prairie dogs do not take away important amounts of grass from cattle or sheep. The prairie dogs eat no more than four to seven percent of the grass livestock would want. Also, cattle, sheep, or horses rarely break their legs in prairie dog holes.

Prairie dogs have sometimes been feared because of disease. They are thought to carry the sickness called the bubonic plague (boo-BON-ick PLAYG). The plague is actually carried by fleas. These fleas can jump onto prairie dogs, but more often, they find a place in the fur of mice, cats, dogs, rats, rabbits, and other animals.

Prairie Dog
FUNFACT:

Prairie dogs are considered a "keystone" species. That means that many other animals depend upon prairie dogs and their towns. Scientists think the dogs are important to more than 180 other animal species.

Coyote

Golden Eagle

Badger

Swift Fox

Black-footed
Ferret

Burrowing Owl

Many species depend on prairie dogs for food and shelter.

Prairie dogs are less dangerous than many other flea carriers. When bitten by infected fleas, prairie dogs usually die within a week. As long as humans do not touch the infected prairie dogs, they will not get the disease from them.

Far from being dangerous to humans, livestock, or wildlife, prairie dogs are important to the health of all. Prairie dogs and their towns offer shelter and food to numerous other grassland species. Scientists think that about 40 species of mammals, 90 species of birds, 80 species of plants, 29 species of insects, 15 species of reptiles, and 10 species of amphibians are connected to prairie dog towns. As the numbers of prairie dogs go down, these other species struggle, too.

A Utah prairie dog looks out over its habitat. It is the smallest of all prairie dog species, with one of the smallest ranges.

The black-footed ferret is now nearly extinct in the wild. Other animals, such as the swift fox, mountain plovers, and burrowing owls, are also falling in numbers as the prairie dog numbers fall.

In 1900, prairie dog populations were thought to total about five billion in North America. Today, scientists consider all five species of prairie dogs to be either endangered (en-DANE-jurd) or threatened (THRET-end) in their survival. However, not all species are listed this way by the government. Some groups still consider prairie dogs as pests.

The future of prairie dogs lies in the hands of people. Learning about prairie dogs and telling others about them are the first steps to saving them. With greater understanding and co-operation, people can protect prairie dogs and their habitats.

By saving prairie dogs, people can also help save the many other animal species that depend upon them. For if the prairie dog goes, so do they.

My PRAIRIE ANIMALS Adventures

The date of my adventure: _____

The people who came with me: _____

_____

Where I went: _____

What prairie animals I saw:

_____   _____

_____   _____

_____   _____

_____   _____

The date of my adventure: _____

The people who came with me: _____

_____

Where I went: _____

What prairie animals I saw:

_____   _____

_____   _____

_____   _____

_____   _____

My PRAIRIE ANIMALS Adventures

The date of my adventure: _____

The people who came with me: _____

_____

Where I went: _____

What prairie animals I saw:

_____   _____

_____   _____

_____   _____

_____   _____

The date of my adventure: _____

The people who came with me: _____

_____

Where I went: _____

What prairie animals I saw:

_____   _____

_____   _____

_____   _____

_____   _____

Explore the Fascinating World of . . .

WILD HORSES

Julia Vogel
Illustrations by Mike Rowe

LONG AGO all horses were wild animals. They ran free in large herds, or groups, across vast grasslands all over the world. In North America's Great Plains, millions of horses once roamed alongside bison, antelope, and other prairie wildlife.

Today, most horses are cared for by their owners. But untamed horses, often called mustangs, still live in remote parts of the American West, far away from most communities. Wild horses also live in a few other places in the United States and around the world. No one brings them food and water or protects them from danger. How do these last wild horses survive on their own?

Wild horses must be able to survive in bitter winter cold and fierce summer heat.

Strong bones and powerful muscles allow wild horses to run faster than any of their natural enemies.

Mustangs belong to a group of large mammals known as the equid (EH-kwid) family. Zebras, wild asses, and burros are also equids. Horses and their close relatives share body features that help them stay alive in open spaces. Long necks help them spot enemies far away, and long legs help them run fast to escape. On each foot, equids have only one toe, protected by a hard covering, or hoof. Hooves help make horses fast and sure-footed, allowing them to stand, walk, and even gallop on their tiptoes.

Almost 60 million years ago, tiny ancestors (AN-sess-torz) of today's equids lived in North America. The fox-sized animals, called dawn horses, ate leaves in swamps and wet forests. As time passed, the climate grew drier and prairies replaced many woodlands. Fossils show that early horses changed, too. They developed longer legs and necks, plus harder teeth that let them eat tough grasses. By about three million years ago, horses looked very much like they do today.

FUNFACT:

Horses run free in many countries, including Argentina, Australia, China, France, Poland, and Canada.

The earliest horses traveled through swampy woodlands on paw-like feet, with four toes on each front foot and three toes on each back foot.

Burros have longer ears and stockier bodies than their horse cousins. Gold miners brought burros to the U.S. as pack animals, and about 4,000 still roam free in the West.

For thousands of years, wild horses crossed land bridges that connected North America to other continents. Horses spread widely across Europe, Asia, Africa, and South America. At the end of the last Ice Age, melting ice packs raised sea levels and flooded the land bridges. The wild horses could no longer cross between continents and had to stay wherever they had traveled. About 8,000 to 10,000 years ago, many large mammals died out in North and South America. Horses, along with mastodons (MASS-ta-dons), camels, and woolly mammoths, vanished mysteriously.

Climate change, disease, and hunting by native people may each have played a part in their disappearance. Whatever the cause, North America's prairies lost their horses.

No one knows where or when people first domesticated (doh-MESS-tih-KATE-ed), or tamed, horses. Cave paintings in France show that Europeans in the Ice Age hunted wild horses for meat. However, by 4,000 to 3,000 B.C., horses in Europe and Asia were valued as work animals as well as for their meat, hides, and milk. People used horses to pull chariots across the grassy plains of eastern Europe and the deserts of the Middle East. Soon the strongest horses were carrying warriors into battle, packing supplies up mountains, and hauling farm wagons. The swiftest horses delivered messages and news faster than ever before. Fast horses were also used for entertainment, including chariot races in the 680 B.C. Olympics.

As people used horses for more and more tasks, they chose the animals that were best at each job and mated, or bred, them to produce even better offspring. Horses were bred to improve qualities such as strength, speed, color, jumping ability, and personality. Careful breeding over the centuries led to the creation of many different breeds, or varieties, of horses. Scientists group all tame horses in the same species (SPEE-sees), *Equus caballus*, just as all dogs belong to the same species, *Canis familiaris*. But the many breeds can look remarkably different. Horse breeds now range in size from the Falabella miniature pony, which may weigh only 31 pounds (14 kg) to the Belgian draft horse, which can reach 2,400 pounds (1,090 kg).

People continued to hunt the remaining herds of wild horses for meat and sport. By the late 1800s, a group of horses in Mongolia called Przewalski's (psha-VALL-skeez) horses were the last remaining true wild horses. A few were captured to keep in zoos, but no one was ever able to tame the fiesty animals. Although the wild herds of these horses died out in the 1900s, groups of Przewalski's horses raised by people have now been set free in Mongolia.

No horses, wild or tame, lived in North America for at least 8,000 years.

When the animals finally returned, they were the tame horses ridden by Spanish conquistadors (kon-KEES-ta-dorz). These strong, swift animals carried the armed soldiers through jungles and across deserts in search of gold. In the 1600s, Spanish settlers raised their tough little horses on cattle and sheep ranches in New Mexico. Some ranch horses escaped to live in the wild. The free-running horses came to be called "mustangs," probably from the Spanish word *mesteño* (mess-TEN-yo), which means stray or free-running animal.

FUNFACT:

The very first horses brought back to America were 16 Spanish horses that landed in Mexico with the conquistadors in 1519.

In the windswept Mongolian grasslands, the wild Przewalski's horse is known as takhi.

Spanish colonists, farmers, and others set horses free on several islands along the Atlantic coast. Though surrounded by salt water, these islands often have little of the freshwater and grasses that horses need to survive.

Some Spanish horses were stolen by Pueblos and other Native Americans. Plains Indians called the unknown creatures "sky dogs" or "elk dogs" and quickly learned to hunt bison and attack enemies on horseback. Trading, theft, and captures from the wild herds helped spread mustangs to northern groups of Native Americans, such as the Dakota and Blackfoot. Many of their horses escaped, too, and the free herds thrived on the lush prairie grasses of the northern plains.

Later European settlers brought different kinds of horses to the prairies, such as heavy draft breeds to pull farm equipment. Some broke free and joined the wild herds. Though the wild horses were no longer all pure Spanish horses, even the mixed-breed animals were usually called "mustangs." The wild herds grew to about two million animals by the mid 1800s.

Throughout the 19th century, wild horses were still often caught and tamed. Captured horses became riding horses, cow ponies, pack animals, and U.S. Cavalry mounts. In the early 20th century, though, people needed fewer horses. They began to value wild horses less. Many argued that the animals were not pure Spanish horses but mongrels, or mixed breeds that were no longer useful or important. In fact, some said wild horses were not native wildlife but feral, or stray, animals that did not belong on the prairies. Some ranchers blamed the horses for competing with their cattle for water and range grass. Some hunters believed that mustangs ate the food of elk, bighorn sheep, and other wildlife they wanted to hunt. Horses were chased off and fenced out of the best grasslands with barbed wire. Thousands were rounded up and sold for pet food or shot as pests. Their numbers fell to 17,000 before they were protected by a 1971 U.S. law. This law banned capturing, harming, or killing free-roaming horses or burros on public lands.

Today, about 50,000 wild horses live in the U.S. and Canada. Some live on private ranches, wildlife refuges, or Native American reservations. A few small groups live on islands off the East Coast, in Georgia, Maryland, North Carolina, Virginia, and Nova Scotia. Most are found on publicly owned land in western states, especially Nevada and Wyoming. Nearly all wild horses live in rugged, dry habitats, or natural environments, where they must work hard to survive.

Because of their harsh habitats, wild horses are smaller than many other kinds of horses. Adults stand about 56 inches (142 cm) high at the shoulder, the height of a tall pony breed. A large male mustang, called a stallion (STAL-yun), weighs at most 1,000 pounds (454 kg). A small female, or mare (MAYR), may weigh only 650 pounds (295 kg). At that size, mustangs grow strong on poor lands where larger domestic horses might starve.

With ancestors from many breeds, wild horses come in many colors and patterns. Most common are different shades of brown, from golden to chestnut to almost black. Horses with brown bodies and black manes, tails, and lower legs are called bays. Black, gray, and tan are other common mustang colors. Roan (ROWN) horses are black or brown with white hairs sprinkled through their coats, and pintos have patches of white and black or brown. A few boldly patterned horses appear to have white blankets with dark spots across their rumps. Those mustangs are called Appaloosas and may be related to horses bred by the Nez Percé Indians long ago.

FUNFACT:

One coat pattern, called Medicine Hat pinto, was especially valued by some Native Americans. They believed the horses' special coat pattern protected the animals and their riders from battle injuries.

The coat pattern of every pinto is unique, and some Native Americans treasured these flashy mustangs over horses of other colors and patterns.

About 150 to 200 horses with scientifically proven Spanish ancestry live in the Pryor Mountain Wild Horse Range of Wyoming and Montana.

A few mustangs have even more unusual markings, with zebra-like stripes on their legs, and a stripe down the spine. These rare horses often have short backs with one less vertebra (VER-tih-bruh), or backbone, than other horses. Early Spanish breeds and other ancient types of horses had these same traits. A group of these mustangs live in the Pryor Mountains of Montana and Wyoming. Blood tests show that these horses are closely related to their Spanish ancestors of 400 years ago. Scientists believe this is because the mountains isolated these horses, or kept them from mixing with other breeds.

Even in the desert, wild horses cannot live far from streams or other sources of fresh water.

The Pryor Mountain mustangs are now carefully protected and are considered an important part of Western U.S. history.

Wild horses need lots of water to drink. In the driest country, they can go two or three days without water. Horses prefer to drink every day, usually about 10 to 15 gallons (38 to 57 liters). In winter, they eat snow or use their hard hooves to break through pond ice. In hot weather, they stay close to water holes and drink more often if possible. Water is so important to horses that droughts (DROWTS), or rainfall shortages, are probably the biggest natural threat to wild herds.

Horses cannot see well close up, so their sense of smell helps them find their favorite grasses.

Horses need food as well as water every day. They are plant-eaters, or herbivores (HERB-uh-vorz). Their favorite foods are grasses, plants with thin leaves and tiny flowers. Other kinds of plant leaves grow from the tip, but grass leaves grow from the base. That means that when horses bite off some grass, the leaves keep growing. After grazing the grass in one area, horses move to fresh pasture. As long as they have plenty of space, wild horses do not overgraze, or harm grass by eating too much of the plants.

Horses eat many kinds of grasses and other plants. Bluebunch wheat grass, Sandburg's bluegrass, and needle-and-thread grass attract them all year. In spring, a mustang may also eat blooms of flowers such as balsam root, or flowering plants such as dandelions and rosy everlasting. In winter, horses must search harder for food. They may nibble the leaves of bitterbrush, rabbitbrush, and other shrubs. If horses get very hungry, they may even eat juniper bark and twigs. An adult mustang eats about 16 to 30 pounds (7 to 14 kg) of food per day.

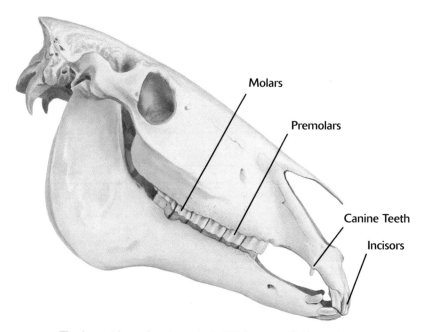

Molars

Premolars

Canine Teeth

Incisors

The largest bone in a horse's skull is its powerful lower jaw.
An adult horse usually has 40 teeth.

Horses bite grass off close to the ground with chisel-shaped front teeth, called incisors (in-SIZE-orz). Flat-topped back teeth, or molars, thoroughly crush each bite. So much grinding wears down the molars, but a horse's teeth keep growing all its life.

Even well-chewed grass is hard to digest. Cattle, deer, and many other plant-eating mammals have four-chambered stomachs that break down their food. Horses have a one-chambered stomach as humans do, but horses also have a special pouch in their intestines (in-TES-tins), called the cecum (SEE-kem), that aids in digestion (die-JEST-shun). Tiny bacteria (bak-TEER-ee-uh) live in the cecum. Once the swallowed grass reaches the cecum, bacteria break it down so the horse's body can absorb the nutrition (new-TRISH-un). This digestive system means that horses can live in dry lands with poor quality grasses. However, they must eat more food than cattle of the same size to get enough nutrition.

Experts can estimate a horse's age by its teeth. Over time,
rough grasses wear down the teeth in specific patterns.

Horses have four natural gaits, or ways of moving: walk, trot, canter, and gallop, which is the fastest.

Whether grazing or resting, wild horses must stay alert for predators (PRED-uh-torz). A mountain lion may be crouching behind a boulder, or a black bear may be lumbering through the trees. If cornered by a pack of coyotes, an adult horse can defend itself with powerful kicks. Predators most often attack foals, or horses less than a year old. A mare could try to defend her young, but usually both run. If the foal cannot keep up, it may be doomed.

Horses are built for speed and nearly always run from danger. A mustang's top speed, 35 miles per hour (56 km per hour), makes it faster than any of its natural enemies. Horses also can leap over obstacles, such as fallen logs or

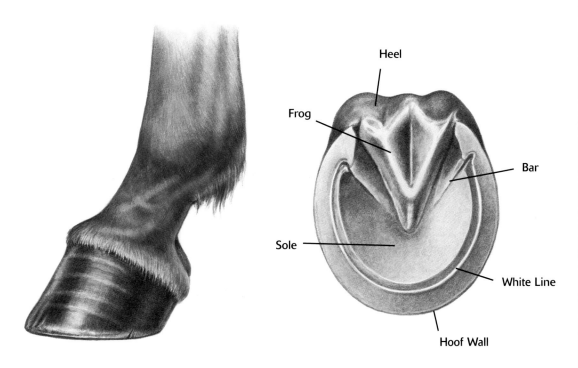

Heel

Frog

Bar

Sole

White Line

Hoof Wall

Like its teeth, a horse's hooves wear down
with so much use but keep growing all its life.

broad ditches, and make sudden turns and zigzags. If a river blocks their way, horses can swim to safety.

Scrambling through rocks, mustangs are amazingly surefooted. At the back of a horse's foot is a wedge-shaped, springy pad called a frog. The frog cushions the hoof and protects the leg as it strikes hard surfaces. The small pad can be life saving, because a wild horse with a broken leg will not survive. With their shock-absorbing frogs and hard hooves, mustangs could outrun a champion racehorse on rocky ground. Mustangs are also famous for their stamina (STAM-ih-nuh), which means they can keep running long after other animals must stop to rest.

Horses rely on their keen senses to warn them of danger. They have large eyes that are very sensitive to movement and can see far into the distance. Positioned on the sides of the head, the eyes take in a broad field of view. A horse can move each eye separately, so the animal can watch in front and behind at the same time. They do not see colors as people do, but they see better in the dark than humans. Horses sometimes seem nervous and jumpy to observers, but their eyes may be telling them of possible dangers humans cannot see.

Horses also have sharp hearing. Their cup-shaped ears collect sound from near and far. Like their eyes, their ears can move separately. A horse can turn its ears in almost any direction without moving its head. If a mustang hears something frightening, it may bolt without ever looking to see what made the sound.

Even these young wild colts use their sharp eyes, ears, and noses to watch out for danger. If any of them spot trouble, all are ready to run.

These wild ponies recognize each other's smell as different from all other horses on Maryland's Assateague Island.

Having a good sense of smell helps mustangs survive in several ways. Their large nostrils detect the scents of unseen predators, especially if wind carries the smell toward the herd. Horses also use their noses to find water and grass, even under deep snow.

One of the most important ways they use scent is to identify other horses. Each mustang has its own smell, and the animals sniff each other's nose and body when they meet. Horses may also smell each other's droppings, which look like fist-sized lumps of mashed grasses. A stallion will leave its droppings at certain spots around its home range, or the area where it lives and feeds. When another stallion comes by, he adds to the droppings piles. Large piles can build up in areas where many horses pass, such as on paths to shared water holes. Scientists think that the piles are a way that stallions challenge each other. Sometimes, male horses meet near the piles to fight.

Wild Horses
FUNFACT:

If a mare does not recognize a foal by smell, she will not let it nurse. Orphan foals are rarely adopted by other mares in the band and will die if they cannot eat on their own and keep up with the rest.

A dust bath will soothe this mare's itchy skin, but too many
of these baths in one spot can kill the grass.

Horses also have a surprisingly sensitive sense of touch. When a biting fly lands on its skin, a mustang reacts fast. It twitches its skin, swishes its tail, and even shakes its whole body to get rid of the pests. Pairs of horses may stand side-by-side, head-to-tail, helping each other swish away flies. To protect their skin and perhaps soothe bites, horses roll in dirt or mud. On hot days when insects are worst, mustangs climb to high country in search of winds to blow the swarms away.

Owners of domestic horses care for their horses' skin by daily grooming, or brushing and combing. Wild horses groom each other. A pair stands together, each partner nibbling the other's mane and coat, especially around the shoulders. Horses groom each other for just a few minutes, but they often stay together afterward. Grooming and other touching seems to help horses get along.

Getting along matters because horses are highly social animals. Mustangs almost always live together, usually in small groups called bands. A typical family band is made up of one mature (ma-TOOR) stallion, one to eight mares, and their offspring under two or three years old. The mares in a family band are often called a harem.

The band stallion constantly protects his family from danger. He often stands apart from the rest, alert while the others graze. Stallions can rarely snatch more than a mouthful of grass or a few minutes of sleep. At the first sign of trouble, the stallion snorts a loud warning.

He may circle the group, nipping at slow mares and foals, hurrying them to join the others. Then the band members dash away, but the stallion stops to look back, ready to fight if necessary.

To a wild stallion, the worst kind of trouble may be another male mustang. Rivals try to sneak up on the band and steal a mare or two, or the whole harem. When a challenger approaches, both stallions prance and toss their heads, sniff noses, paw the ground, and squeal. Usually after less than a minute, one horse gallops away, defeated. Such sparring teaches the stallions in an area who is strongest.

Wild Horses
FUNFACT:

A stallion is usually not powerful enough to take over a band until at least age five.

170

Stallions use teeth, hooves, and bodies as weapons during short, fierce battles. The winner rounds up one or more mares and takes them away.

Serious fights are rare, but if neither horse backs off, a fierce battle breaks out. Both males rear back on their hind legs and strike out with their front hooves. They lunge at each other, biting at legs, sides, and necks. This pawing and turning kicks up so much dust that it is hard to see the action. These battles are noisy, with angry neighs (NAYZ) and dull thuds whenever their bodies slam together. At last one horse gives up, leaving the other with the band. Each may have bloody wounds, torn ears, or other scars that last a lifetime.

This band has spread out to graze, but all will fall into line behind the lead mare when she decides it's time to move.

During the battles, mares often graze quietly nearby. The outcome seems to matter little to the band. Mares have their own leader, an older female who is almost as bossy as the band stallion. The lead mare gets to drink first at water holes and picks where the band eats each day. When the stallion snorts an alarm, band members instantly follow the lead mare to safety. All trust her to choose an escape route that is fast but not too difficult for the youngest foals. Their lives depend on her knowledge and quick thinking.

The whole band must communicate well to keep safe. Horses make several kinds of sounds. Each horse has a unique call, or neigh, that other band members recognize. Mustangs also whinny, a loud call that can be heard far away. If one horse gets separated from the rest, it whinnies and listens for the band to answer. When any horse snorts, the others lift their heads and watch out for danger. But a soft nicker reassures the other animals that all is well. A nicker is a quiet, throaty noise like a soft chuckle. Mares use nickers especially as tender greetings for their foals.

Wild Horses
FUNFACT:

Horses can sleep lying down or standing up. Their legs lock so they can relax without falling over.

Alert   Sleepy   Angry

A horse's ears, eyes, and nostrils help communicate its mood to other band members.

Body language also helps mustangs communicate. Feet, tails, and ears give clues to mustang moods. Stomping a front hoof is a mild warning, telling others to step back. Holding up a back hoof declares, "I am about to kick!" Normally, a horse's tail hangs down in a relaxed position. An excited horse may lift its tail into the air as it trots or prances. If a horse nervously flicks its tail back and forth, it is a sign of anger.

A horse communicates with its ears, too. An alert horse pricks its ears forward or turns them back and forth. A sleepy horse's ears droop. If the ears flatten back against the horse's head it means the mustang is angry and may bite or kick.

A foal nurses while its mother stays alert to danger. A mare almost never gives birth to more than one foal at a time.

Mares do not always get along, but they rarely leave the band. Stallions may let mares go off alone to give birth. Sometime in April, May, or June, a mare ready to give birth looks for a quiet spot hidden from mountain lions and other predators. The foal arrives feet first. The new mother nuzzles it, getting to know its smell, and nickers softly. Soon, the newborn starts untangling its stilt-like legs, struggling to stand. A healthy foal stands up within an hour of birth and soon nudges under its mother's belly to nurse, or drink its mother's milk. Any foal too injured or weak to walk will be left behind when its mother returns to the band.

Adult horses usually only run when startled, but foals like this one run to build muscles and to play with other foals.

A young male horse is called a colt until it is four years old, and a young female is called a filly. Newborn colts and fillies weigh around 66 pounds (30 kg). Like adult mustangs, their coat colors and patterns vary. Mare and foal rejoin the band a day or so after the birth, sticking close together. The foal nurses several times a day at first, but it starts nibbling grass at three to four weeks. By its first winter, most of its nutrition comes from grass. Mares usually wean, or stop nursing, their yearling offspring shortly before new foals arrive the next spring.

Throughout their first year, colts and fillies play hard. They race each other, kick up their heels, and nip at their parents and older siblings. Sometimes, their play annoys older band members. Then the foals clack their teeth, a sound that seems to say, "Sorry! Please don't kick me!" Their rough play helps the foals grow strong. Perhaps even more important, they develop close relationships that hold the band together.

Wild Horses
FUNFACT:

A horse's height is often measured in "hands." One hand is equal to 4 inches (10 cm), and an adult mustang usually stands about 14 hands (142 cm) at the shoulder.

A filly stays with her family until she is one or two years old, when an outside stallion usually steals her away. After fillies leave and join new bands, many have their own foals by the next spring. The band stallion usually chases a colt out of the band when the young male is one or two. Band stallions do not welcome new colts, and the young males are not yet strong enough to take over bands of mares. Instead, they join another kind of horse group called a bachelor (BACH-ler) band. Bands of 2 to 12 young male mustangs stick together for safety and comfort.

The bachelors lead carefree lives. Like other mustangs, they spend much of each day and night seeking food and water. But unlike band stallions, they have time to rest and play. Sometimes they chase other bachelors as if they were harem mares. Or they rear and paw the air at each other in mock battles. Such play helps them build skills they will need to take over their own family bands in the future.

These three bachelor stallions are dun colored, a common coat pattern for wild horses with Spanish mustang ancestors. They live together in Oregon's Kiger Horse Management Area.

Even if a stallion like this pinto has only one mare, he guards her constantly.

Bachelor bands and family bands sometimes join into a large herd. Usually, herds gather briefly in areas with good grass and plentiful water. Young males keep to the edges, while band stallions watch them nervously and keep their mares tightly bunched. Within the herd, some stallions rank above others. Bands with the most powerful males get the best grass and the first chance to drink at water holes. In the past, herds sometimes included thousands of horses. Today few areas have enough wild horses to form herds of even 100.

In large and small groups, mustangs' lives are shaped by the seasons. Every spring foals arrive, and mares mate again just days after giving birth. Summer brings blazing heat in prairies and deserts, and the animals must find ways to stay cool. They roll in cool mud at water holes and rest in the shade of any trees or boulders they can find. They also must stay alert for wildfires, using their noses to test the wind. A sniff of smoke warns, "Wildfire! Run!"

Wild horses do not migrate long distances between summer and winter territories. Instead, many migrate to different elevations, climbing up or down, depending on the season. In summer, they seek cool breezes and fresh grass by climbing to mountain meadows. They walk to get water in the coolest parts of the day and graze more often at night.

Wild Horses
FUNFACT:

In the past, the biggest mustang herds lived in Texas.
Some early Texas maps had large areas simply
labeled, "Vast herds of wild horses."

The first snowfall is a sign that the wild bands should move to sheltered pastures.

By fall, horses are growing thick coats for cold-weather protection. Bands come down from mountains or high ground to wind-sheltered valleys. The first snows bring hardships, forcing mustangs to dig for food and break ice for water. Older horses remember where to find grass and shrubs, and foals follow them, learning where to look and how to dig. During the winter, bands spend nearly all their time just finding enough to eat. Blizzards may drive the horses to huddle together behind evergreen trees for warmth, and ice storms may prevent them from eating at all. By spring, the survivors' ribs show through their patchy, shedding coats. All are eager to taste the first green shoots of spring grass.

Despite their hard lives, mustangs have long life spans. They can live over 20 years in the wild. A family band's mares may stay together until they die. A band stallion, though, only stays as long as he can drive off challengers.

Thick coats help this yearling (left) and its mother survive winter in the Pryor Mountain Range. The mare's rounded belly shows she may be expecting a new foal in the spring.

Defeated older stallions do not join bachelor bands but live alone. Unless they can steal or win new mares, these stallions never father offspring again. Without other horses for companionship and safety, they may not survive long.

With long life spans and with most mares having new foals every year, wild horse herds can grow quickly. In fact, they can double in size in four or five years. Too many grazing animals could harm the horses' dry habitat because it kills grasses, erodes soil, and pollutes streams with churned-up mud and droppings. The worst overgrazing can cause desertification (de-ZERT-if-ih-KAY-shun), or the changing of rich grassland into unhealthy desert.

This young foal must feel safe enough to lie down and rest.
Soon it will be up and running free again.

Mustangs share the range with over four million livestock and two million antelope, elk, and other large wild animals. Ecologists, or scientists who study natural systems, are working to learn how horses and other plant-eating animals affect the land.

Are there too many wild horses? To prevent overgrazing, a federal agency called the Bureau (BYUR-oh) of Land Management studies herd size on public lands. Herds that the Bureau thinks are growing too fast are rounded up, and many of the horses are offered to the public for adoption. Unwanted horses, often older animals, may be released again or sent to live on private mustang sanctuaries (SANK-choo-air-ees), or protected places.

Roundups, though, are expensive and can frighten or injure horses. A better solution may be to give mustangs a kind of medicine that reduces their ability to have offspring. The horses do not need to be rounded up to get the medicine, making controlling horse populations less expensive and less stressful for the horses.

Like other prairie animals, mustangs need open spaces. Wild horses are symbols of freedom, reminders of Spanish explorers, bold Native Americans, and dashing cowboys. Most of all, they are free creatures, adapted to life on their own. Mustangs do need our help, though, to make sure there are always wild lands where they can run free.

My PRAIRIE ANIMALS Adventures

The date of my adventure: _____

The people who came with me: _____

_____

Where I went: _____

What prairie animals I saw:

_____   _____

_____   _____

_____   _____

_____   _____

The date of my adventure: _____

The people who came with me: _____

_____

Where I went: _____

What prairie animals I saw:

_____   _____

_____   _____

_____   _____

_____   _____

Internet Sites

You can find out more interesting information about prairie animals and lots of other wildlife by visiting these Internet sites.

www.buteo.com	Birds of Prey at Buteo.com
www.wildmustangs.com	Black Hills Wild Horse Sanctuary
www.blm.gov/education/00_resources/articles/wild_bunch/index.html	
	Bureau of Land Management
www.kidsplanet.org	Defenders of Wildlife
http://www.desertusa.com/dec96/du_pdogs.html	Desert USA
www.enchantedlearning.com	Enchanted Learning.com
www.ggro.org/idhelp.html	Golden Gate Raptor Observatory
www.horse-behavior.com/index.html	Horse Behavior
www.nationalgeographic.com/burrow/	National Geographic Society
www.nationalgeographic.com/kids	National Geographic Society for Kids
www.nwf.org/kids	National Wildlife Federation
http://nature.org/	The Nature Conservancy
www.pbs.org	PBS Online
www.peregrinefund.org/Explore_Raptors/index.html	Peregrine Fund
www.savewildhorses.org/kidspage.htm	Wild Horse and Burro Freedom Alliance
www.worldalmanacforkids.com	World Almanac for Kids Online
www.worldwildlife.org	World Wildlife Fund
www.yptenc.org.uk/	Young Peoples Trust for the Environment
http://nationalzoo.si.edu/publications/zoogoer/1997/5/equidprimer.cfm	
	Zoogoer

BISON Index

HAWKS Index

PRAIRIE DOGS Index

WILD HORSES Index

Our WILD™ WORLD SERIES

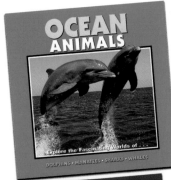

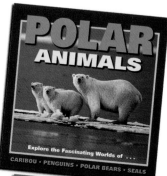
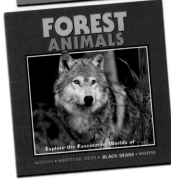

Look for these Big Books in the Our Wild World Series:

OCEAN ANIMALS
ISBN 1-55971-781-5

BIG CATS!
ISBN 1-55971-798-X

POLAR ANIMALS
ISBN 1-55971-832-3

FOREST ANIMALS
ISBN 1-55971-708-4

REPTILES
ISBN 1-55971-880-3

APES AND MONKEYS
ISBN 1-55971-863-3

See your nearest bookseller, or order by phone 1-800-328-3895

NORTHWORD PRESS
Chanhassen, Minnesota